TEACHER
HAIKU

TEACHER
HAIKU

Three Short Lines for
Your Long School Year

RANDY HOWE

Illustrations by
Nelle Davis

life

Guilford, Connecticut

An imprint of Globe Pequot Press

gpp®
life

GPP Life is an imprint of Globe Pequot Press.

Text design by Sheryl P. Kober
Illustrations by Nelle Davis © Morris Book Publishing, LLC

Library of Congress Cataloging-in-Publication Data is available on file.

ISBN 978-0-7627-5279-9

Printed in China

10 9 8 7 6 5 4 3 2 1

Introduction

Haiku has long been popular with educators. It can be used to teach kids about poetry, syllables, synonyms and "juicy words," nature, culture in general, and Japanese culture in particular. *Teacher Haiku* is not, however, a book for teachers to use with their students. It is a book *for* teachers; a book dedicated to those who educate kids on a daily basis. I am a teacher, so I understand what a limited resource time is. After a busy day of teaching, it isn't easy to muster the energy to read a newspaper, magazine, or book. A vignette of seventeen simple syllables is perfect for those running on empty and who knows? On a good night, we might be able to read three or four haiku before passing out!

Just as a report card is a snapshot of a student's performance, a haiku is a snapshot of an emotion or event. Every classroom is host to thousands of events and emotions over the course of the school year, so the connection between these two art forms—education and haiku—is clear. Summarizing a student's performance in as few words as possible isn't easy, yet somehow, with every report card, we do it. We find a way to provide insight, each of us a poet in our own right.

Teacher Haiku is one-hundred-and-eighty-plus days of school, told in one hundred poems. I recommend that you read from beginning to end, starting with the final sighs of summer and ending with those last glorious days of school. In between, there are parent conferences and discipline issues, professional development days and due dates, assemblies and standardized tests. Some haiku will make you laugh out loud; some, simply nod your head in agreement. Hopefully, each and every one will further add to the passion you already feel about your chosen profession. Teaching isn't an easy job: it can be all-consuming. So, when you find the time to read, treat yourself to a haiku or two. Enjoy the opportunity to relax and reflect. In seventeen, simple syllables: I know that you deserve it.

Randy Howe
Madison, CT

A Lesson on Haiku

Before there was *haiku*, there was *tanka*. This was poetry written in praise of gods and monarchs, and it was tanka that first made use of a 5-7-5-7-7 syllable form. Like those "attention grabbers" we try to get our students to write, every great tanka began with a strong *hokku*, which means "starting verse." Hokku writers held a privileged position in Japanese society as they were the literary equivalent of lead-off hitters. After their 5-7-5 piece, a second writer would compose the final two 7-7 verses, but by the nineteenth century those fourteen syllables had disappeared, and haiku as we know it was the dominant form of poetry in Japan.

Not all English-language haiku poets follow this seventeen-syllable format. When they choose to follow a more loosely constructed, short-long-short format it is called "free form." One reason these poets prefer free-form is not the ability to write more; it is actually so that they can write less. (Some will write in a 3-5-3 style while others challenge themselves in 2-3-2.) This is because translators will tell you that it takes just eleven Japanese syllables to convey as much information as seventeen syllables of English. On the other hand, it is easier to write haiku in Japanese as, grammatically speaking, the order of the words doesn't alter meaning as much as it does in English.

Take, for example, the following haiku:

> To teach young children
> a hurricane or rainbow
> a calm in the storm

In English, the placement of the words in the final verse is critical. "A storm in the calm" obviously has a much different meaning than "a calm in the storm." What teacher wants to be the storm when he or she can be the calm? It is also worth noting the ambiguity of this haiku: the subject isn't necessarily the teacher as those young children might be the hurricane, the rainbow, or the calm for the teacher. Good haiku speaks to the individual while also leaving itself open to interpretation. This haiku will mean different things to different teachers. It might even mean different things to the same teacher, depending on the kind of day he or she had.

In a perfect world, the teacher is a rainbow for the students, leading them to the pot of gold that is learning; most amazing of all is when that favor is returned.

Notice how that sentence lacks the poetic punch of the haiku. I have said too much; I've been too direct and painted a metaphorical picture that is a bit too dramatic for the advanced reader. What I lost in resonance, I gained in cheesiness! The haiku poet, no matter what language he or she is writing in, does not want to write a sentence, let alone a run-on sentence like this one. Also, punctuation is avoided as often as possible. There are many rules in the writing of haiku, but they aren't intended to be debilitating. As Japanese-American haiku poet Keiko Imaoka warned, "By concerning ourselves too much with the outward form of haiku, we can lose sight of its essence." That is one thing that hasn't changed since the time of the first great haiku poets, writers like Basho and his teacher, Yoshitada: respect for the essence of haiku. In that regard, the haiku poem is like the lesson, the haiku poet like the teacher.

Gulls screech "Buh-bye beach"
Noise soon replaced by students
Where's my aspirin?

Bathing suits, flip flops
I shall miss you all. Hello
slacks, shirts, socks, and shoes!

The alarm clock laughs
a hideous "Ha! Ha! Ha!"
School should start at noon

Supply closet's stocked
if all my students need is
water-logged journals

Huge desk, wrong place, no
help to be found—looks like it
will have to stay put

Three new computers
Great news except for one thing
Where are you, keyboards?

Classroom is ready
Moved all my boxes. Next stop?
The chiropractor

The first day of school
Students' anticipation
matched only by mine

New rules every year
student and teacher handbooks
Well meant, never read

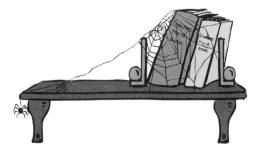

Syllabus can be
a four-letter word when due
in less than one week!

Social promotion
Only knows thirteen letters
but first grade it is

Curriculum map
is a road to frustration
with this committee

School elections or
popularity contest?
Democracy lives

Twenty-six students
and a budget freeze this year
Thank you, taxpayers

What retirement fund?
Six dollars all that is left
after bills are paid

Every kid asks if
I need more wrapping paper
It's fund-raising time!

Election Day means
staff meetings from 9 to 3
I vote we stay home!

Twenty pairs of ears
stick out like question marks so
why won't they use them?

"Art on a Cart" is
much more like "Mess on each Desk"
Smocks almost stay clean

Signed permission slips?
Somewhere in my room or worse,
forgotten at home

Fallen leaves become
autumnal art for class walls
Glue fight means calls home

Harvest Fair and I
put the T in PTA
Bobbing for apples

Meet the Teacher Night
"Welcome!" Smile at their long legs
under little desks

Report cards are due
Of Kenny Can't-Sit I write
"Aggressive learner"

Report cards are due
Of Miss Know-It-All I write
"Very self-assured"

Pre-fab comment list
Feedback reduced to cliché
"A pleasure to have…"

Conference nightmare
Parents wander the hallways
NO maps to be found

Raise the grade? I should
just give her a B because
Mom is a lawyer?

The memorable
ones thrill us and wear us out
all at the same time

His mother calls me
I bid a fond farewell to
my prep period

A new job hazard:
highlighters and pen ruin
every pair of pants

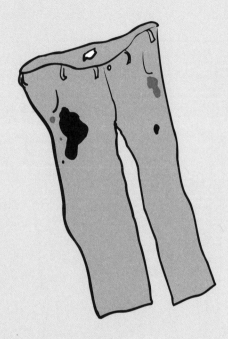

New student arrives
No records, no grades, no clue
Come on in, young man!

Pencils in ceiling
I ask them for the truth but
no one is talking

I'm supposed to be
well-read and well-informed but
when is there the time?

Crazy mom e-mails
nonstop. Time to pretend the
system's down again

Pajama Day is
my favorite. Teaching in
slippers is pure bliss

Birthday cake no more.
Allergies, obesity
We sing then eat grapes

Winter wonderland
Complaining, coughing, sniffles
for them, then for me

Holiday pageant
Can't wait for the choir to start
Did I sit on gum?

Lost art of passed notes
Salutations, penmanship
Text messaging rules

Snow day happiness
Gift of pajamas and peace
Grading or TV?

I buy the school lunch
and mourn the leftover shrimp
left on my counter

February love
Make sure every kid in class
gets cards and stickers

Grocery cart filled
bulk-sized hand sanitizer
My war against germs!

She draws a rainbow
and says "This is for you." Oh
how I needed that

love,
Amonda

No more protocol?
Support staff and observers
enter unannounced

Staff lounge fridge home to
science experiment food
I'm not cleaning it!

Principal will ask
even though she knows I can't
handle one more thing

If I give feedback
and students don't listen do
I still make a sound?

Monday's lesson plan
somehow lost in cyberspace
Curse you, computer!

Answer sheet, booklets
state assessments — kids want to
cry and so do I

How many teachers
and degrees does it take to
fix a paper jam?

Vacation next week
Failing kid is away now?
Great plan, mom and dad

Back from vacation
A smell from my desk: Yogurt?
I fear mouse droppings!

Document all things
on Forms One, Two, Eight, and Ten
Schools love to kill trees

At exactly noon
"Cough!" then laughter because that
trick never gets old!

Time for Science Fair
Papier-mâché volcanoes
Bottle tornadoes

Kids copy and paste
essays — maybe I could write
my thesis that way

Murphy's Law again:
cold coffee welcomes me back
after the fire drill

School nurse determines
"Chocolate is medicinal"
Entire staff cheering

Friday happy hour
I need sleep but fight the yawns
with cold beer, hot wings

Bus duty? Really?
Twenty years of teaching, now
I direct traffic

The longest month, March
Might be time to use all of
my saved-up sick days!

Evaluation
says it was a great lesson
I agree and sign

Rubric be damned: Mike
turned his project in on time
A-plus for effort

After school Friday
empty classroom is all mine
Turn up the music!

Show and Tell: Amy
shares her spelling bee trophy
then spells "elation"

Some days teaching kids
to read is like painting a
house with a crayon

I do love children
but oh how I long for my
bed and a good book

Raining outside means
raining inside; ceiling drips
puddles on my desk

Certification
Test, a Saturday wasted
Get me out of here!

Students talk nonstop
except when I ask for class
participation

Disaggregated
data useful to know but
dryer than chalk dust

This meeting has gone
on longer than root canal
I miss my students

Young teacher's fab style
confirms my fears: I've become
the sweater lady!

An apple a day
keeps the doctor away but
it's coffee we want!

Kids love class pets but
both fish died, ferret stinks, and
snake has gone missing

Two plus two equals
four rowdy kids and one big
headache during Math

Answers to every
question and lots of advice
Thank God for mentors

Editorial
questions teacher salaries
How original!

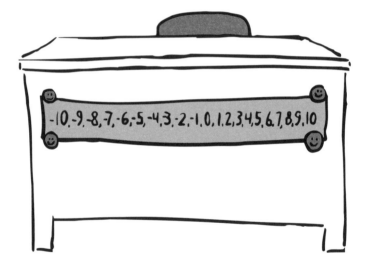

Number sense makes sense
once I can help the kids make
sense of the numbers

Rhyming, phonics, sound-
symbol association
Thank you, Dr. Seuss!

Favorite lesson:
they sit criss-cross apple sauce
I read a story

Crayon drawings and
scribbled sentences. How I
love writer's workshop!

Three bags of prizes
from the school store: extrinsic
rewards work wonders

Students back from gym
hyper as can be. Bad news:
standardized test time

Music class today
How can I grade with all this
singing in my room?

Why is it so rare
that we find time to sit and
talk with our colleagues?

Assembly begins
A whoopee cushion echoes
One of my students?

At cocktail party
My students' exploits the hot
topic of the day

Lesson plans ignored
Substitute teacher didn't
do one thing I asked

The tables have turned
Homework is more work for me
than it is for them

She burps then giggles
Contagious laughter ensues
How can I be mad?

Lesson plans are due
but it is Sunday and the
sun calls out my name

Radiator is
an oven by the window
cranking heat till May

I will never be
too harried or too old to
chaperone a dance

Today is Field Day
Let them run, jump, dance, and sing
One month till summer!

Windows wide open
The breeze and lawn mower's buzz
Teachers daydream too

Staff meeting at 3?
Oh what a cruel punishment
Let's just meet next year!

Adios, farewell
I will miss you, ex-students
Woo hoo! Pass the wine!!!

Acknowledgments

First and foremost, a nod of appreciation to my editor, Mary Norris, for all of her encouragement and guidance. She taught the teacher, and I thank her for all her efforts.

Next, a shout out to colleagues past and present. Seventeen syllables could never sum up the respect I have for the hard-working, kid-inspiring, curriculum-following, parent-communicating, young teacher-mentoring teachers at Putnam/Northern Westchester BOCES, the Micro-Society Magnet School, and The Sound School.

And finally, a big ol' thank you to my wife, Alicia Solis. She is the first editor I have for every project, and words cannot describe how much I appreciate her very objective feedback.